BLACK COUNTRY PUBS
IN OLD PHOTOGRAPHS

BLACK COUNTRY PUBS
IN OLD PHOTOGRAPHS

COMPILED BY

ROBIN PEARSON
AND JEAN WADE

Budding
BOOKS

A Budding Book

First published in 1991 by Alan Sutton Publishing Limited

This edition published in 1998 by Budding Books,
an imprint of Sutton Publishing Limited
Phoenix Mill · Thrupp · Stroud · Gloucestershire GL5 2BU

A catalogue record for this book is available from the British Library

ISBN 1-84015-034-3

**To the
drinkers, guvnors and brewers
of
the Black Country**

Typesetting and origination by
Sutton Publishing Limited.
Printed in Great Britain by
WBC Limited, Bridgend, Mid-Glamorgan.

CONTENTS

ACKNOWLEDGEMENTS

The authors would like to thank all individuals and organizations, not forgetting licensees and fellow drinkers, who assisted in this compilation. Particular thanks are due to:

Bob Binns
Pat Burford
Mrs Dalton
Eric Doyle
R.G. Fullelove
Mrs Greenhough
Harry Harrison
Roger and Vanessa Hill
Mary Mills
Mr and Mrs L. Palfreyman
Alan H. Price
David Radmore
Liz Rees
John Wilkinson

Tim Batham of Bathams Brewery
John Crompton of the Black Country Museum
Malcolm Timmins of Darlaston Local History Society
Tony Price of Mitchells & Butlers
Frank Power Commercial Photography
John Maddison of Smethwick Local History Society
Ned Williams of Uralia Press

County Express, Stourbridge
Smethwick Photographic Society
Tipton Camera Club
Walsall Observer

Dudley Local History and Archives
Sandwell Local Studies
Walsall Local History Centre
Wolverhampton Archives
Bilston Library
Brierley Hill Library
Stourbridge Library
Wednesbury Library

Also, thanks are offered to all the many individuals who over the years have contributed photographs to their local archives.

INTRODUCTION

For many years the public's conception of the inn, tavern or pub was probably summed up nationally in the words of a poet born in Halesowen. William Shenstone (1714–63), who lived at the Leasowes, produced a poem entitled *Written at an Inn*, the last seven lines of which run:

> *Through rain or shine, through thick or thin,*
> *Secure to meet, at close of day,*
> *With kind reception at an inn.*
> *Whoe'er has travelled life's dull round*
> *Where'er his stages may have been*
> *May sigh to think how oft he found*
> *The warmest welcome – at an Inn.*

Another local writer closely associated with a Walsall pub was Doctor Samuel Johnson (1709–84). Not only did he produce a brief biography of William Shenstone, he offered his own observation on the pub with the typical wit which he applied to all life's ups and downs: 'There is nothing which has yet been contrived by man, by which so much happiness is produced as by a good tavern or inn.'

Life, however, in the early days of the industrial exploitation of the Black Country had a more grim edge to it. The Victorian novelist David Christie Murray, who was born in a house on West Bromwich's High Street, was to describe that life in his many novels. 'Sanded floor, huge open fireplace, blazing with an enormous fire, after the generous-looking fashion of the mining districts, where coal is cheap and a good fire is counted first of household comforts.' This was Murray's description of a Black Country inn thinly disguised in his third novel. It was perhaps a little nearer to the truth than the idealized version of a pub found in Shenstone's musings.

Nearly 150 years ago large areas of the Black Country remained essentially rural in character. The first industrial revolution had sought to exploit the natural resources, coal and iron. In line with the enclosure movement, a nationwide process, tracts of open space were developed. In some areas the objective was not really agricultural improvement, but the development of villages into towns. The pub landlord of those days often combined the job of farmer with that of publican. In that combined capacity there was an opportunity to use land adjoining the pub for the building of houses. In Darlaston publicans took the lead in providing much needed housing for the workers of the second industrial revolution. Even in the late nineteenth century landlords were erecting housing. Roland Ray, the enterprising licensee of The Pheasant Inn in Oldbury, put up a row of houses in nearby Pottery Road, while on the other side of the Black Country William Lloyd Roberts of The Barley Mow was building houses which survive today on Penn Common.

Prior to the early nineteenth century most Black Country pubs were either small alehouses or more sophisticated coaching inns. After the Beerhouse Act of 1830 there was a massive expansion in the availability of drinking establishments. This in part coincided with the expansion of many local towns. Traditional industries such as nail making were giving way to heavy engineering – foundry workers were soon to earn the reputation for the consumption of vast quantities of ale. The erection of pubs close to factories was exemplified by the building of Wolverhampton's Parkfield Tavern to serve the workers in nearby foundries, and the naming of The Soho Foundry Tavern in Smethwick. Another Smethwick firm, Fox, Henderson & Co. of the London Works, gave local pubs the opportunity to attract customers by calling inns London Works and The Crystal Palace. Numerous pubs called The Jolly Collier, and some The Jolly Nailer, were earlier attempts at the retention of customer loyalty.

Many pubs were houses adapted as licensed premises or built to blend in with the small properties found in rows of side streets, where the Black Country was, according to a writer in 1868, 'faithfully portrayed in every building and every human face.' Only later, in the 1930s, did pubs seek to dominate their surroundings as estate after estate of pre-Second World War housing swept over most of the remaining 'plains of heaven', Murray's description of the region's green fields. Brewers erected large roadside establishments which almost mirrored the grandeur of the old original coaching inns, even to the extent of being set back from the line of the road to create the illusion of accommodating the modern stage coach, the motor car.

The vast, almost municipal feeling of that 1930s architecture serves as a reminder of the grandeur of the Victorian and Edwardian pubs, whether it be The Bear in Bearwood or the enormous Prince Albert which still stands proudly within Wolverhampton's encircling ring road. Pubs such as these were built by the new generation of corporate brewers.

The euphoria that followed the passing of the 1830 Beerhouse Act, when anybody who paid the modest licence fee could open a pub, gave way to changing social and economic conditions. The brewery companies saw a means of increasing their manufacturing base by offering licensees finance to expand the business but at the same time ensuring a 'tie' that gave them more and more control of the drinkers' environment. So called 'Victorian values' called for hard work and a sober social life and the temperance movement and chapels sought to reduce the number of pubs. Breweries also responded to the edicts of the licensing justices to improve the condition of the facilities. Large ornate interiors gave the drinkers a feeling of luxury that could not be found at home.

In some ways the Black Country survived the worst excesses of brewery merger mania. Local breweries run by generations of families were eventually taken over by regional brewers with strong local traditions. Amid all this commercial activity, small 'independents' and 'home brews' have continued to operate and have been supplemented by localized big brewing operations to give the customers a fine choice of real ale at competitive prices. It is that beer which brings in the customers. Closeness to home has always been the advantage of the Black Country pub. Willenhall and Bilston seemed drinkers' paradises with pubs every few yards. In Oldbury it was 'an ability test' to drink half a pint in every pub in Halesowen Street and its convenient side streets. A once favourite pub crawl was up and down Spon Lane, West Bromwich to Smethwick and back, with a choice of twenty-two pubs *en route*!

Good landlords were essential 'ter keep folks 'appy in the plerce.' Many a Black Country pub was known by the guvnor's name – not only a sign of affection but perhaps an indication of a reputation for well kept ale. Prior to the population explosion and industrial expansion of the region, when many landlords combined farming with inn-keeping, only the larger inns with a passing coaching trade could afford to support a full-time licensee. At Wednesbury George Loxton ran The George and Dragon on strict and efficient lines, to the extent that the establishment was popularly called 'Loxton's'. In common with a number of Black Country publicans, he was teetotal and a strong supporter of Methodism. The longevity of many licensees gave a certain sense of stability to the 'werkin' mon's parlimunt'. This was further underlined by many a widow continuing to run the pub after the death of her husband. Often son followed father behind the pumps or in some cases, such as at The Elms in Aldridge, daughters followed in their father's footsteps.

The pubs in this industrial area still fulfill their essential role in the local community as more than just a place selling ale – they are, in fact, a great Black Country institution.

THE PLUMBERS, Tyndal Street, West Bromwich in about 1919. John Pedley was licensee for over thirty years.

SECTION ONE

Famous and Infamous

While Black Country pubs cannot boast that 'Queen Elizabeth I slept here' they have their associations with the famous – and the notorious. In other cases the building itself was to attract fame.

National figures such as John Wesley and Doctor Samuel Johnson had links with local pubs. The boxer, William Perry, Champion of England 1850–57, trained for his prize fights using The Fountain in Tipton. Later he kept his own Black Country pub. Many an ex-footballer has followed a national trend for sportsmen to acquire licensed premises.

Some pubs had a less savoury past, being connected with rogues and vagabonds. The forger William Booth kept up a legitimate business front in a West Bromwich pub. Occasionally villains took advantage of a pub's location on or close to a parish boundary to evade the attentions of the legal forces from their own district. Bradley's Lamb and Flag acquired the dubious nickname of the 'Hell House' while Wednesbury's Olde Leathern Bottel provided at one time a seemingly safe haven for coiners from Walsall crossing the brook at Wood Green.

Other pubs gained a regional if not national reputation in the hearts and minds of drinkers. Netherton's Old Swan, affectionately known as Ma Pardoe's, and nearby Himley's Glynne Arms, now officially The Crooked House, have become attractions in their own right. Everyone probably knows Brierley Hill's Vine by its nickname of The Bull and Bladder where beer is enjoyed under Shakespeare's updated quotation.

THIS BRADLEY PUB stood in Salop Street on the boundary between Bilston and Coseley, and shared responsibility made it difficult for the local constables to enforce the law. Cockfighting, dog fights and fisticuffs between customers led to the pub's nickname of the 'Hell House'.

ALDRIDGE'S IRISH HARP, dating from the late 1600s, was the birthplace of Tom King, the highway man associated with the more infamous Jack Sheppard and Dick Turpin.

WILLIAM PERRY, champion prize fighter between 1850 and 1857, used the above Tipton pub as his headquarters. Perry, better known as the 'Tipton Slasher', later became a publican himself.

MARIA TATE was licensee of The Old Still, Wolverhampton in 1896, while her husband James conducted a prosperous wine and spirit business from these premises. Their daughter, later Dame Margaret Teyte, was to become an internationally famous soprano, charming audiences around the world from 1906 until 1955.

A TUNNEL REPUTEDLY RAN from this Restoration inn to Willenhall's St Giles' church. Mrs Kay held the licence from 1922 until 1970. Still with its original cellars, this pub has been described as 'exceptionally well preserved.'

THE OLD RED COW IN SMETHWICK. Taken within a month of each other in 1936, these two photographs show the front and the side views. By 1937 the pub had been demolished and rebuilt further north up the High Street.

THE WHITE LION, DARLASTON. In 1743 John Wesley was taken from magistrate to magistrate by the 'Wednesbury Mob' who objected to his preaching activities. They stopped here for refreshment on a very wet evening *en route* to Bentley Hall where magistrate Colonel Lane showed the same lack of interest as his fellow justices. The disused malt house at the back of the pub doubled as a Drill Hall for the Darlaston Volunteers and meeting place for civic leaders in pre-Town Hall days. The pub was also the boyhood home of Harmer Nicholls, later Lord Peterborough, father of *Coronation Street* star Sue Nicholls.

THE RING O' BELLS in West Bromwich in about 1898. The animal pound in front gave rise to the local saying that beer was 'sold by the pound'. The pub was demolished in 1971 for a road widening scheme, with the pound being preserved and moved a short distance to Church Vale.

THE VINE, BRIERLEY HILL. Doris May Batham stands on the steps. The butchers on the left side of the building gave the pub its nickname, 'Bull and Bladder'. On the front cover Arthur Joseph Batham, husband of Doris, is in the centre of a later photograph taken at a time when Daniel Batham held the licence. Arthur, grandfather of the present head brewer, Timothy Batham, held the licence himself from 1939 to '44.

THE STONE CROSS INN, West Bromwich. By the beginning of the century the original cross had already been replaced with a signpost which doubled as a gas lamp.

AN EARLIER VIEW OF THE STONE CROSS INN with its red sandstone cross still in place. William Martin was landlord for twenty years from 1872. Later, the licence was held by Mrs Anne Martin, who could be the lady standing in the doorway.

THE SCOTT ARMS, built as a Georgian coaching inn, was a prominent feature of Great Barr life. Its brewery used water from its own well, inquests were held in the pub, and there was even a mortuary in one of the outbuildings. In the large barn at the back of the pub, seen in the lower photograph, local Roman Catholics held services prior to the building of their own nearby church. The pub, pictured above in 1900 and below in 1954, was replaced in 1966 (see p. 77).

THE GLYNNE ARMS, Himley was once called the 'Siden House' from the effects of mining subsidence. It is now known by its second nickname, the 'Crooked House'. Even as early as the 1890s it had become a popular tourist attraction, particularly at weekends and on summer evenings.

BILLY MEIKLE, the Walsall photographer, did much to record the old pubs of his town. Here, sitting far right, he relaxes with his friends in Lichfield Street's British Oak, later a Twist's Brewery house.

THE OLD HORNS, Queslett developed the tradition of serving free cuts of beef to its customers on New Year's Eve during its 200 year history. The pub also acted sometimes as a venue for coroner's inquests. It is pictured here in 1963 prior to its demolition. The pub was rebuilt further back as part of a road widening scheme.

AN EXAMPLE OF TWO MAJOR BREWERIES IN IMMEDIATE COMPETITION in West Bromwich's Seagar Street. The pub on the left was known as the 'Fourpenny Shop', then the price of a pint of beer! The neighbouring Hare and Hounds, built in 1797 and rebuilt in 1897, provided a base for the more legitimate business activities of William Booth, the notorious forger who was 'twice tried, twice hanged and twice buried.'

THE DARTMOUTH, once West Bromwich's premier pub, was the centre of the town's business and social life. Local courts were held here until 1851. Former licensees included ex-Albion star Harry Clements and also William Isaiah Bassett, WBA chairman at the time of the 1930/31 FA Cup win. The pub was demolished after its closure in February 1977.

THE MOLINEUX, a name generations of football fans have associated with their local team, Wolverhampton Wanderers. Founded in 1887, the club began to use The Molineux as a dressing room two years later. Built by a family of local merchants who later drastically altered it by putting a new front at the side to have country instead of town views, Molineux

was sold in the 1860s to Oliver Edgar McGregor. He then converted it into licensed premises. Seen here in about 1875, the rear terraced gardens became public pleasure gardens, which now form part of the grounds of the Wolves Football Club.

THIS EARLY PHOTOGRAPH taken in about 1875 shows the Hill Top pub opposite Trotters Lane halfway through the ownership of Thomas Griffiths who was 'licensed to brew'. Appropriately an earlier licensee, John Sheldon, had the additional occupation of pig dealer.

YE OLDE LEATHERN BOTTEL, rebuilt in 1913, can in fact claim to be Wednesbury's oldest pub as the original dated from the early sixteenth century. A former coaching inn which served at one time as a magistrates court, it also became a safe haven for 'coiners, thieves and other felons' fleeing from the Walsall constables.

WALSALL'S WHITE HART at Caldmore was originally built as a residence for the Hawe family on the site of an earlier half-timbered house. It was only in 1801 that it became licensed premises. Today it stands boarded up with an uncertain future.

THE OLD STILL HOTEL. Once the oldest pub in Walsall's town centre at 34 Digbeth, it was associated with a famous literary figure. Part of the interior was called Dr Johnson's Corner after Samuel, who rested between coaches on his visits back to Lichfield. Billy Meikle (see p. 21) described The Old Still as 'very old and original, it was a Tudor building.' This photograph shows its late Georgian front with the Victorian bay windows.

THE SARACENS HEAD AND FREEMASONS ARMS HOTEL. Named to commemorate the Crusades and still known by some locals as the 'Napper', this old coaching inn acquired the addition to its name when the local Freemasons Lodge established its headquarters here. It was also a meeting place for Dudley's Nonconformist leaders. Former licensees include Julia Hanson's father John Mantle, and appropriately her brewery later acquired the premises. Next door, solicitor William Henry Tinsley had premises in part of the former Roebuck pub.

THIS TIPTON PUB at the corner of Hurst Lane and Sedgley Road West was demolished and rebuilt about 1923 as The Doughty Arms (named after a local politician and member of the licensing justices). Today it rejoices in the more widely known name of Mad O'Rourke's Pie Factory, and is seen here about 1904 when William Bates offered 'Home Brewed Ales'.

MA PARDOE was a teetotaller but her Netherton pub hardly needs an introduction to drinkers — it was one of only four home brewers remaining in England before the real ale revival.

THE GREYHOUND AND PUNCHBOWL, High Street, Bilston, formerly part of a manor house built in the mid-fifteenth century, only became a public house in 1820. Even at the time of Joseph Wheeler's licence it showed signs of the dilapidation which led to the eventual restoration of the building in 1936.

Inside and Out the Back

No two pubs are alike inside. There might be a 'corporate image' introduced by the brewery, there may well be a conscious attempt to be basic or luxurious, but the glory of pubs is that every one is different.

Whenever the design of the interior is changed there are customers who feel it has been carried out with sympathy and others who think the entire concept a travesty of what was there before.

One local brewery has recognized just what it is that many people want from their pubs, and have opened a successful chain which has in effect reverted to basics. They offer a straightforward public house, where customers are able to enjoy a traditional pub game, or a quiet drink with good food, free from the intrusions of electronic music, games machines or an overpowering 'theme'.

Drinkers tend to be attracted to a pub by the smartness of the frontage. If it is changed or altered in any way it is usually done to uniform design. Only the back of the building may reveal in its hotchpotch lack of uniformity something of the history of the pub that would be otherwise missed by the casual observer. Apart from the smaller country inns, which sought to gain trade with gardens and tables, some town pubs did have a few benches 'out the back' – nowadays nearly every backyard is adorned with chairs and umbrellas.

CURIOS GALORE IN THE FOX INN, DUDLEY.

NINETEENTH-CENTURY LANDLORD MARTIN PERRY FOSTER SENIOR doubled as a file maker using this workshop at the rear of his family's Spread Eagle in Darlaston. The pub at No. 50 Cramp Hill was demolished in the late 1950s.

THE NEW HOP POLE, West Bromwich in the 1930s with Christmas decorations.

THE SAME ROOM after alterations in the early sixties. The screen on the left in the top photograph has been removed but the central pillar remains, and the cash till is in the same position to the right of the smoke room door.

CUSTOMERS AT THE BACK OF PELSALL'S RED COW IN ABOUT 1900.

HIGH BACK SETTLES shown alongside the fireplace and staircase of The Red Cow, Smethwick in 1933, a few years prior to demolition (see p. 15).

THE NEWLY OPENED SHIRELAND INN, Smethwick, 1 December 1924. Its licence was granted on the conditional closure of two nearby pubs, The Bell Inn and The Vine Inn.

CHILDREN PLAY in the yard of Walsall's historic Old Still in February 1958.

THE SMOKE ROOM OF THE CAPE OF GOOD HOPE, Smethwick. Note the 1920s style greenery.

INSIDE THE SHRUBBERY, Horseley Road, Tipton in 1939. Above, the smoke room, and below the gents only smoke room.

TWO SETS OF TAPS ON THE BAR OF THE THIMBLE MILL INN, Smethwick, which opened in April 1928. The pub was built opposite the site of the former mill which for more than 150 years was used in turn for grinding corn, making thimbles and cutting files, finally finishing its working life in the mid-1880s as a corn mill once again.

COSY INTERIOR OF THE HAWTHORNS, Blackheath, also in April 1928.

A BACKYARD LEADING TO THE STABLES AT WEDNESBURY'S RED LION in February 1965. A former coaching inn, it became a stopping point for omnibuses running six times daily to Birmingham and Wolverhampton in the nineteenth century. The front of the building was more memorable for its appearance on a painting depicting the Wesley Riots of 1743.

THE PALM COURT APPEARANCE OF THE LOUNGE OF THE BARLEYCORN, Smethwick, newly opened on 6 April 1939 (above), contrasts with the more utilitarian interior of The Springhill, Penn, photographed the previous year.

A DOG AND CAT JOIN THE STAFF in the yard at the rear of The Farriers, Queen Street, West Bromwich at the beginning of the century. The pub was rebuilt within the Queen's Square shopping development, but ceased trading in the late 1980s.

THE CLUB ROOM OF THE LONDONDERRY, Basons Lane, Oldbury, which opened 16 July 1930.

CUSTOMERS HAVE HELPED RAISE THOUSANDS OF POUNDS FOR CHARITY by paying to see that a ball will roll *up* a shelf at The Crooked House, Himley, a former 1700s farmhouse. (See p. 21).

ASSEMBLY ROOM AT THE GEORGE, Oldbury, 16 December 1937.

INSIDE THE QUEENS HEAD, Brunswick Park Road, Wednesbury. This new building had been erected alongside the original Queens Head and opened on 15 January 1937. The old pub is shown on p. 115

LICENSEE ELIZA STEVENS with her daughter Nellie in the pre-1924 Turks Head, West Bromwich. This Sams Lane pub had very finely ornamented beer taps compared with the

other pubs in this book. Thinly disguised as 'The Saracen's Head', the interior of this pub
was vividly described in the Victorian novel *Joseph's Coat*.

THE ABBEY, Abbey Road, Smethwick, which opened on 2 October 1931. The table in the centre of this wonderfully light room appears to be set for a meal for two.

THREE PEOPLE RELAX IN THE SUN and feed the pigeons in the back yard of The George Hotel, once Walsall's most famous coaching inn. This view shows the original eighteenth-century building, which was replaced in the 1930s. (See p. 70.)

Landlords

Publicans – This is Yoher Life
(written 1970)

by Off the Cuff . . . Black Country Poet

I bet them in pubs cud write a book
'un it cud be called 'The Sittin' Duck'
'cus the job ay just servin' drink
it ay uz saft uz yoh mite think
theer's lots uv pints they've gorra lern
ter keep beer un folks uz they doh tern
if the mild ay rite or the bitter's dull
they'me uz bad uz the beer they pull . . .

Aer' kid it teks a level yeddid fella
ter keep things rite down in the cellar
if the pipes ay clear oda pal it's theer
it soon shows up in the beer
then yo'le get sum lift it by the lite
tellin all un sundry 'it ay rite'
wotever sort uv trouble's brewin'
'gaffers must know just wot they'me dewin'.

They must bottle the feelin's uz yoh know
wen they lissen ter the terls uv woe
if it's in the bar or in the smoke
they've gorra gi' un tek a joke
if the tork is law, sex or sport
they've gorra mix wi' evry sort
a sort uv judge un jury all in one
'cus they'me sp'ozed ter know wot goz on ...

They'me 'one uv the best' or 'one uv the wust'
wotever they dew they woh cum fust
they must try ter keep a smilin' ferce
ter keep folks 'appy in the plerce
they must carry on wen they'me 'arf jed
un still must keep that level yed
'cus if they doh un they cum unstuck
the yed's on the block fer 'The Sittin' Duck'!

Harry Harrison

A WARM WELCOME FROM LANDLORD SIDNEY HADEN at The Woolpack in 1937, at the time Dudley's oldest pub, claiming a continuous licence since 1622.

THE GENTLEMAN IN THE DOORWAY is probably William Howell, who was licensee from around 1904 until 1911, and whose name is on the wall, partly hidden by the pub sign. Officially named The Bradford Arms, this Darlaston pub was nicknamed 'The Fying Pan' for many years, and the 'Fryin' Pon Club' met here on Sunday evenings. Part of the building dated from the late 1700s and demolition became necessary in the early 1980s. The new pub, built next door, is now officially called The Frying Pan.

THE LANDLORD LINES UP UNDER HIS NAME outside the Hall End Tavern in this once outlying area of West Bromwich in about 1900. With him are, from the left, his son-in-law Tom Deamer, his daughters Ellen Horton Deamer and Elsie Horton and his son Herbert Horton.

WEST SMETHWICK LANDLORD GEORGE STAMP, a former Chance's glassworker, in his new role as landlord of The Grapes.

GLADYS SMALL on 8 November 1980, receiving gifts at the party to mark her retirement as manageress from The Little Barrel, Dudley.

TEN YEARS EARLIER, on 1 January 1970, she stands by the barrels which on that day gave the last beer from the wood. Once part of The Eagle Tavern, the pub became known as The Little Barrel in the 1870s. Alterations were carried out in the mid-1980s. On the shelves, cigarettes are priced at 5s. 2d. and 2s. 7d.

TESTIMONIAL & TRIBUTE TO THE LATE

Mr Tom Griffiths

OF THE — LOWER GORNAL — FOUNTAIN INN

Presented to His FAMILY

3 Daughters
2 Sons
18 Grand-children
6 Great-Grand-children.

He had the English mans love for horses — & he loved his game of bowls — & the companionship of his fellow men

By His Numerous FRIENDS And CUSTOMERS.

Who desire to shew Their Respect & Sympathy

To him as a True Sportsman & Gentleman for he shewed these Qualities in every sphere of his Life : in all Circumstances and Environments

As gentle as a lamb at home As a Lion in the chase.

The type of MAN who contribute to a Nation's greatness :

He was interested in every kind of Sport and He excelled in the Noble Art of self-defence especially. Even aspiring to the Amateur Championship of England in the YEAR 1892 He even sparred with the redoubtable WORLD CHAMPION. JACK JOHNSON He won also A GOLD MEDAL for entering a Lion's cage at a Fairground at Dudley

A Man whom the Gods favoured with Honesty, Strength, Courage & Loyalty. He held a blameless record as a Licensee for 50 YEARS & the iron hand in a velvet glove was the Index to a well kept Inn. he could be gentle : he could be tough. His Friendship was Sincere & he possessed a Character of which any Englishman might be proud Born at Gornal in the Year 1869 His brilliant career was closed 1947

He was keenly interested in Church Services at Lower Gornal Saint James Church : together with his belov'd Wife who passed away in the Year 1941 : United on Earth, now united in the Life Beyond They seek the World of Glory together Sic Transit Gloria Mundi InTuas Manus Domini

He was also Vice-President of the Gornal Branch of the British Legion.

AGED 78 YEARS

THIS GLOWING TRIBUTE TO TOM GRIFFITHS was painted in 1947 by John Humphries, a Gornal bricklayer. It hung on an inside wall of The Fountain in Temple Street, Lower Gornal until the relinquishment of the licence by the Griffiths family. The interior of the pub has recently been refurbished.

A CONTRAST IN DRESSING STYLES with Thomas William Whittaker (above) at the entrance to The Nelson in West Bromwich's New Street, and Samuel Bolton (below) outside The Rose Inn on Wednesbury's Union Street. In very small lettering above his name it says Samuel was 'not to sell on Sunday.'

ALFRED MOSES DABBS stands outside his pub. Various members of the Dabbs family kept pubs and traded as beersellers in the Hill Top area close to Wednesbury.

LANDLORD JAMES FOSTER'S STAFF AND CUSTOMERS line up outside Bearwood's old Kings Head in 1898.

JOSHUA COX'S FAMILY poses outside what was known as The Gate, which he kept at Hurst Hill, Coseley in the last years of the nineteenth century. From the 1900s onwards the pub was called The Old Gate and was kept for a good few years by William Tranter. Pubs which stood in an area where a tollgate had been on a turnpike road were often called The Gate or, as in the case of the pub almost opposite this one, The Gate Hangs Well. Both pubs were later rebuilt and set back allowing Gorge Road to be widened. The new Old Gate was built in 1937, its brewing tradition continuing for a number of years after this.

ARTHUR AUCOTT OF THE HEN AND CHICKENS, Langley, May 1950. With him, looking at a sample of the inn signs exhibition, is Mrs G.W. Rose, Mayoress of Oldbury.

BREWING BROTHERS BENJAMIN AND THOMAS WOODHOUSE owned many local pubs and are seen here in the doorway of The Alma, Hall Street, Dudley. Originally The Travellers Rest, the pub was renamed in 1861 after an 1854 Crimean battle. Benjamin held the licence from the beginning of the century, with the brothers' Alma Brewery to the rear. They bought the nearby Victoria Brewery in 1914, changing its name also to Alma.

WILLIAM HULME, landlord of Wednesbury's Ye Olde Leathern Bottel, shares a joke with a customer on 2 February 1965.

MR AND MRS CHARLES BONE AND FAMILY including their young daughter Mary outside The Yew Tree on the corner of Rycroft and Stafford Streets in Walsall. The pub closed down about 1930.

IN THE LATE NINETEENTH CENTURY AT ANOTHER YEW TREE in Albion Road, West Bromwich, landlord James Downing was issuing tokens made by Fenwick of Birmingham. Tokens were generally issued for a lower denomination, usually 3d.

A NEIGHBOUR WATCHES MRS EDITH PARSONS, landlady of The Railway Tavern at 113 Birmingham Street in Stourbridge, face the camera.

THE WAGGON & HORSES in Hall Street, Dudley, originally a beerhouse, had closed by the end of the nineteenth century. Wine merchants Henry Plant & Sons also owned a number of pubs in Bilston.

BRADLEY LICENSEE MRS LOUISA O'BRIEN stands with her daughter Lettice on the steps of No. 33 Wesley Street in 1928. Known locally as the Stores, the pub closed down in the 1960s.

SECTION FOUR

Going, going, gone

Just as the origins of public houses are widely varied – alehouses, coaching inns, or those built specially for the refreshment of workers in nearby mines and foundries – so the end of the line for licensed premises is reached for many reasons too.

Sometimes a building, or part of it at any rate, was so old that there was no other course but to pull it down. Many pubs stood in the way of planned development such as road widening schemes or housing programmes. In both these cases a new pub was often built as near as possible to the original site. Even at the turn of the century The Bear in Bearwood was dismantled and rebuilt a few feet further back in line with the new road.

Some pubs were delicensed. The licensing justices might have felt the pub had become redundant as it had lost so much trade, or decided to sacrifice the licence to make provision for another pub. This happened particularly in Smethwick in the 1930s with the advent of the large estate pubs such as The Thimble Mill and The Two Brewers.

Once a pub had been delicensed it might have been sold as a private residence. More often, demolition was its final destiny, sometimes only after having been left to become gradually derelict.

THREE EXAMPLES of what can happen to pubs. Top left: The Acorn, Kings Hill, delicensed thirty years ago and now gone. Top right: Dudley Arms, Wolverhampton, sold for shop conversion in January 1958. Bottom: The Talbot, Walsall, demolished March 1963.

THE END OF TWO WOLVERHAMPTON PUBS. Above, The Crown and Cushion bites the dust in Bilston Street. Below, the demolition of The Swan and Peacock on nearby Snow Hill.

THE GEORGE, WALSALL, originally built in 1781, was twice demolished, first (above) for rebuilding in 1935 and secondly (below) in 1979 to make way for shops and offices. The earlier building's importance as a major Staffordshire coaching inn was reflected by the addition of the front entrance columns in 1823 which were obtained from the earlier dismantling of Fisherwick Hall near Lichfield. The statue of Walsall's heroine Sister Dora stood resolute throughout the proceedings.

THE END OF THE ROAD for this High Street pub in Quarry Bank.

DEMOLITION OF THE SEVENTEENTH CENTURY ROYAL OAK, Daw End. The replacement pub erected at the rear was the second post-war house opened in the Walsall area by the owners Butlers.

THE KING EDWARD VII in Ablewell Street, Walsall, closed in January 1963 and demolished in March 1964 to make way for a petrol station.

DEMOLITION OF WEDNESBURY'S HISTORIC GEORGE AND DRAGON HOTEL, which was licensed from 1814, in January 1965. Apart from the handy location for market traders, many famous members of the acting profession stayed there during the days of local live theatre.

WEDNESBURY'S GEORGE AND DRAGON may have been older than its licence if the date on the beam held by demolition foreman Joe Harris is to be believed. The hostelry was called 'Loxtons' in those days after the first licensee. A prosecution under the then newly introduced Weights and Measures Act against George Loxton was dismissed – he had been accused of selling beer in too large measures!

DURING THE DEMOLITION the workers found a large round cellar which may have been used for services before greater religious tolerance allowed Methodists to build the nearby Spring Head chapel. A more sinister use of the cellar may have been for dog fights and ratting contests. As well as the cellar, a large catchpit to hold rainwater was discovered.

THE DOG AND PARTRIDGE, Darlaston had been closed in 1966, and four years later Councillor E. Wainwright stands outside surveying the derelict frontage. Ownership had passed to the council and there was concern at vandalism.

INSIDE THE DOG AND PARTRIDGE the dust-covered piano stands as mute memorial to times past. Below, bottles lined up on the bar by local children gave ample opportunity for target practice.

ANOTHER LONE PIANO stands as a reminder of happier days in the ballroom of Wolverhampton's Star and Garter, demolished in 1964. This picture was taken in 1961.

THE BEAR AND RAGGED STAFF was originally built in 1815 as a residence for the master of the Walsall pig market. As a pub it was first called The Corporation Arms, with a six day licence. It closed in February 1966 and along with other buildings in the High Street was demolished five months later. The demolition firm hired the local fire brigade's turntable ladder to ensure the safety of its workers.

TO THE EXTREME LEFT OF THE ORIGINAL SCOTT ARMS BUILDING in Great Barr are the temporary licensed premises provided for use during its forthcoming demolition. In its place was to be a shopping centre, a new road layout – and, of course, a new pub.

THE DEMOLITION IS ALMOST COMPLETE by 10 May 1966. Various items such as lamp posts, traffic lights, and a bus stop and shelter are visible in both pictures. On the right is a clearer view of the barn described on p. 20.

BUILT TO COINCIDE with the extensive residential development of West Smethwick in the middle of the nineteenth century, The Waggon and Horses stood on the corner of Oldbury Road and Nine Leasowes. This last street was called Pleasant Street when first built in 1826.

THE PUB IS BEING DEMOLISHED to make way for newer premises in January 1967, almost seven years after the picture opposite.

THE BRADFORD ARMS, on the corner of Upper Bridge Street and Lower Rushall Street, Walsall. The pub closed in November 1932 and is now the site of a garage. Note the lack of scaffolding and safety notices.

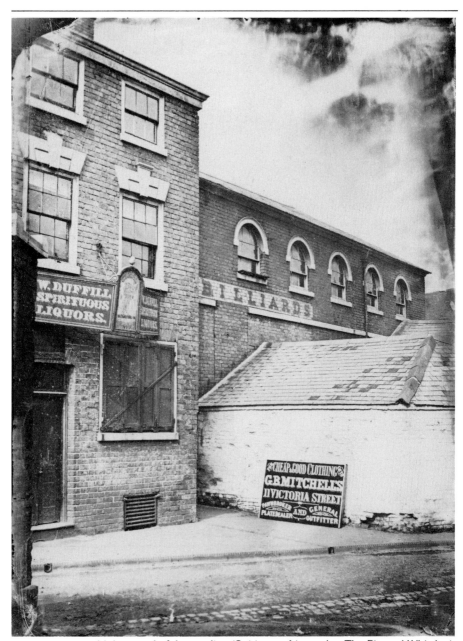

WILLIAM DUFFILL sold the wonderful-sounding 'Spirituous Liquors' at The Pig and Whistle, in the very narrow street called Wheelers Fold off Princess Street, Wolverhampton. At this time it was common practice for pawnbrokers to put their signs outside various premises to indicate a forthcoming auction of the more valuable goods, such as jewellery, which had not been redeemed.

THE ROYAL EXCHANGE INN, Leabrook, on the Tipton side of the old boundary with Wednesbury, pictured here in August 1968, had been delicensed some fifty years earlier. The last licensee was Fred Shinton before the pub became the home of the Blythe family. The carts belong to Arthur Blythe who operated as a 'general trader' from here prior to the eventual demolition of the old inn.

KNOWN FOR MANY YEARS AS 'THE WIDDERS', because it was kept by a widow, this late 1970s shot of The Miners Arms in Owen Street, Tipton shows the pub in its last few years. Soon afterwards it was closed and left to become derelict until finally succumbing to demolition at the end of the 1980s. The pub's former official name was The Round of Beef.

THE FINAL DAYS OF WALSALL'S OLDEST PUB (see pp. 28 and 37). Demolition is in progress on a rainy April day in 1959.

ONE OF DUDLEY'S OLDEST COACHING INNS was already closed in April 1929, with posters advertising the auction of its furnishings. It was later demolished and is now the site of a bank on the corner of High Street and Union Street.

SOMETIMES PUBS WERE DELICENSED, as in these two examples. The appropriately named Railway Tavern in Great Western Street, Wednesbury (above) became a private house. West Smethwick's Plough Inn is pictured below in June 1935 for sale as freehold property.

WEDNESBURY'S FORTUNE OF WAR, suffering its own misfortune, stood at the corner of Wellcroft Street and Trouse Lane.

SECTION FIVE

Old World Charm

Photography came just in time to capture views of pubs and people before the coming of the motor car. These old pictures show a world so very different from our own, one in which time seemed to have stood still. The presence of the photographer often caused all those who noticed him to stand and stare.

There is a timelessness about these places which emphasizes our present day view that this was an era of charm and grace. Picturesque quaintness of town centre pubs, mostly in Wolverhampton, contrasts with The Elms, an old coaching inn in Aldridge, and the matter-of-fact bulk of The Malt Shovel in Great Barr. Others such as The Dog and Partridge in Walsall, looking quaint, were established to serve a particular working community, in that case the local metal workers.

THE ELMS in High Street, Aldridge, pictured in about 1904, was described by a local journalist as 'the social centre of the village.' Its licensing hours were from 6 a.m. to 11 p.m. and it was also open on Sunday afternoons 'for the benefit of visitors.' Mr Letts was the licensee, and he was followed by his daughter Mrs Street, and then her sister Mrs Rhodes. Their brother Mr Ben Letts, seen here outside the pub, kept the baker's shop next door. The Elms was demolished in 1954.

THE OLD BARREL on the corner of Victoria and Bell Streets, Wolverhampton in 1876. Mrs Elizabeth Bee later took over the licence.

THIS PHOTOGRAPH OF THE FOUNTAIN INN was taken in New Street, Wolverhampton about 1880 at the time of Thomas Hyde's licence.

A SPLENDID TURN OF THE CENTURY STREET SCENE on Piper's Row, Wolverhampton. Many pubs were called The Staffordshire Knot after the heraldic device used by the county's leading noble family. A nineteenth-century Lord Stafford undertook property development at the top end of nearby Darlington Street.

THERE WAS A WELL ESTABLISHED METAL WORKING INDUSTRY in Walsall by 1760, and The Dog and Partridge in Sandwell Street was one of several pubs which served the metal workers. It was rebuilt in 1968.

THE FREEMASONS ARMS stood in the Horsefair (today's Wulfruna Street), Wolverhampton in 1879. At the time the town's first major slum clearance was being carried out in an area which also included Lichfield Street and Caribee Island. The pub's licensee was Thomas Fullard.

THE ELEPHANT AND CASTLE at the corner of Cannock Road and Stafford Street, Wolverhampton in 1876. It was replaced by an equally tall building complete with model elephant and castle.

THE QUARTER HOUSE, named after the custom of landlords collecting their tenants' quarterly rents here, lay on the busy Compton Road. This 1910 view shows a locality then outside the main town area of Wolverhampton. The spire in the background belonged to Trinity Methodist church, now gone, but the pub survives as a modern building.

THOMAS MARSH HELD THE LICENCE OF THE MALT SHOVEL on Newton Road, Great Barr at the beginning of the century. The huge barn at the side was probably used for the home brewing business. The pub was later demolished for road widening and rebuilt further back.

THE STAR AND GARTER in Victoria Street, Wolverhampton, rebuilt in the early 1800s, soon became an important social centre. It was the venue for the Florist Society, and saw meetings of Wolverhampton Cricket Club and the Licensed Victuallers' Association.

SECTION SIX

From Beerhouse to Palace

Apart from ancient and historic inns, most Black Country pubs originated as beerhouses at a time that coincided with a period of industrial expansion. In 1830 the Beerhouse Act was passed in an attempt to restore ale to its rightful place by suppressing the worst effects of 'madam gin'. The parallel suppression of cruel sports involving animals left a public with a need for diversions from the equally cruel realities of early nineteenth-century industrial working life. For a small sum anyone who could brew in his or her own house was allowed to sell beer to the public with the provision of minimum facilities.

In rows of side streets many terraced cottages sold beer. Two houses knocked together or the addition of two bay windows on the ground floor saw the transformation of many ordinary houses into typical Black Country locals.

Architectural grandeur characterized pubs built at the height of the Victorian age. Pubs such as Wolverhampton's Prince Albert competed with its neighbouring industrial buildings. Others like The Brown Lion in Pleck had a saddleback roof with parapet gables to emphasise its importance. The pub, as opposed to the traditional inn, had evolved from a basic beerhouse into a prominent building in its own right.

THE COTTAGE SPRING, Darlaston (left), and (below left) The Great Western on the border of Black Lake and Swan Village, West Bromwich both started life as beer-houses. Below right, The Riflemans Arms, Wollaston, Stourbridge, has reverted to being a private residence.

BRIDGEMAN STREET, WALSALL was developed as part of a large housing programme in the 1850s. It is probable that two of these houses were converted into a pub about ten years later. The Globe Inn served as a pub for a hundred years until its closure.

THE PARKFIELD TAVERN, Parkfield, Wolverhampton was built in the early 1800s for the use of workers from the nearby foundries. At the time of this photograph Isaac and Elizabeth Johnson were selling 'strong old ale'. The pub's smoke room was to the right of the main entrance, next to the private house at No. 716.

THE LAMP, Foundry Street, Darlaston, seen here in 1961 with little to distinguish it as a pub except the board above the front door, was a good example of a one-roomed pub. Foundry Street no longer exists, but there is a recently built pub, Aladdins Lamp, in nearby Wiley Avenue South.

THIS TEMPLE STREET, WEST BROMWICH PUB, owned by a Smethwick brewery, was an almost identical version of its namesake in Harvills Hawthorn (see p. 101).

THE LANDLORD OF THE LION, Great Bridge was described for many years merely as a 'beer retailer'. The premises to the left at Nos 60–64 were those of G. Hipkins, Black Country meat merchants. The wording on the wall read 'pork pies and sausages'.

THE PRINCE CONSORT, New Invention, Short Heath in January 1953. A Banks's brewery dray waggon is approaching from the right.

WALLBROOK'S BUSH INN originated as a home brewed alehouse to cater for the colliers working at the local Coseley pits. Robert Joseph Mahon was landlord at the time of this 1959 photograph of the pub which once stood in Wallbrook Road. From 1880 to 1940 the licence was held by various members of the Price family, their trade listed as 'beer retailer'.

A PUB WHICH HAS A MORE PURPOSE-BUILT APPEARANCE, with its smoke room to the left and presumably its bar to the right, is pictured here in Harvills Hawthorn in the 1930s.

LANDLORDS OFTEN COMBINED PUBKEEPING with other businesses even as late as 1900, about the time of this photograph. Joseph Cole, the aproned landlord to the left of the doorway, ran the Corngreaves Hotel in Cradley Heath and also founded the saddlery concern. His wife

is standing on the step. Joe Cole, Joseph's grandson, continued the saddlery business at nearby 82 Graingers Lane until about 1970.

TWO EXAMPLES of licensed premises being built as extensions to rows of existing cottages. Above, the Prince of Wales on West Bromwich High Street was built over the original cottage garden area. Below, a similar front extension at Hill Top was further enhanced with fascia board, once a popular device of the breweries.

THE WILLENHALL DOOR LOCK FIRM of Beddow & Sturmey Ltd is at the far end of the little lane to the right. The town was famous for its lock-making industry and abounded in small factories – and in pubs in close proximity to them.

UNLIKE MOST OF THE BUILDINGS on the previous few pages, this Walsall pub pictured in August 1963 was built with a large bar and lounge, which were once served by its own brewery.

THIS SMETHWICK HOTEL, although erected earlier than many beerhouses, has an appearance befitting its status on the town's High Street. The photograph was taken on a Sunday morning, 13 July 1930.

AN ORNATE EXTERIOR, even to the extent of a clock over the now blocked doorway, adorns this Pleck pub in the ownership of Walsall's once independent brewery. Built over a hundred years ago, its ceramic decorations were of a sufficiently high standard to gain the pub an entry in an official survey of local buildings in 1985.

WOLVERHAMPTON'S INDUSTRIAL IMPORTANCE at the close of the Victorian age is reflected in the grandeur of some of its drinking establishments, such as the one above, in North Street. Below, in Railway Street, Eley's Staffordshire Brewery had just completed The Prince Albert, a structure sufficiently imposing to compete with the 'fortress-like' appearance of the neighbouring Chubb's Works (to the right).

A BUSY STREET SCENE at the beginning of the Edwardian era in 1902. The splendid pub is The Bear, one of the oldest in Bearwood. There had been pubs on this site since the early 1700s. Work is being carried out to allow for road widening and the provision of tramlines, during

which the pub was rebuilt seven feet further back from the road. The present day building was completed in 1907.

THIS PUB in Cheapside, Wolverhampton, pictured in the 1930s, combined the attractions of wine lodge, smoke room and luncheon bar. 'Dock glasses' are advertised on a window – these were large glasses for wine tasting. Also advertised is Stone's Stout, a product of Bents' Brewery which was in Stone, Staffordshire.

THE TALBOT HOTEL was built in 1845 and once dominated Oldbury's Market Square. Pictured in October 1966, it was closed three years later and finally demolished in 1970.

THE CORNER HOUSE at 210 High Street, West Bromwich, on the Queen's Street corner, had a solid, reassured air. It was at the point which is now the High Street entrance to the King's Square shopping mall.

TWO MORE SPLENDID CORNER PROPERTIES. The Criterion (above) in Lichfield Street, Wolverhampton, the site chosen for Britain's first experimental traffic lights in 1927. Below, Smethwick's opulently named Crystal Palace in Cranford Street in its dying days in 1964. The nearby London Works of Fox, Henderson & Co. had produced most of the ironwork for Sir Joseph Paxton's magnificent structure which housed the Great Exhibition of 1851.

Rural Retreats

The popular misconception, particularly among outsiders, of the Black Country as a vast 'smoke-stained' landscape has always been belied by the reality of a 'most exquisite green fringe', in the words of a nineteenth century local journalist. A quick glance at a map of the region reveals a large number of heaths and greens. Even today there are areas of open space and communities still with a rural feel about them.

Some pubs in this section were still in the country at the time when the photographs were taken. Since then the urban sprawl has engulfed them. The Queens Head in Wednesbury once fronted a green while The Saltwells Inn survives in a green oasis with the spa buildings long since gone or overgrown.

Many pubs doubled as farms, such as The Globe in Pleck and The Pheasant in Oldbury. The latter establishment was quick to develop itself as a place to go out to, especially on summer evenings. Seats and tables were provided in the rose garden to attract people to walk along the country lanes. Other attractions included a rifle range and a skittle alley.

Parties were catered for at Penn's Rose and Crown while the nearby Mermaid at Wightwick offered teas and encouraged cyclists. It was almost as though the pubs were pre-dating the present trend to develop Black Country tourism.

THE MERMAID of Wightwick on the outskirts of Wolverhampton, ahead of its time with teas and tourism, attracted many families and cyclists into the country. Notices to the left and right of the main entrance announced 'To The Tea Room' and 'Cyclists Provided For', and there was a bowling green on what is now the upper section of the car park. The smithy is just visible on the left.

A BLACK COUNTRY ATTEMPT to match the prestige of other health spas had met with little commercial success. At the time of this photograph G. Flavell was running The Saltwells Inn which overlooked the surviving bath buildings.

TWO EXAMPLES OF A FEELING OF THE COUNTRY IN THE TOWN. Above, a 1931 view of The Dog Inn, Smethwick. Below, ten years earlier, Ellen Elizabeth Martin came to the end of her twenty years as licensee of The Queens Head Inn near to Wednesbury's Brunswick Park, pictured here during her tenure. At the turn of the century it was common for people from Wednesbury town centre to take a Sunday evening stroll along Wood Green to this popular family pub.

THE BOAT became a popular name for pubs in the late 1700s with the development of canals. In this view the road runs from the direction of Wolverhampton and on towards Thomas Telford's Staffordshire and Worcestershire canal, built in 1766. Beyond the pub are

THERE WAS A BARLEY MOW INN on Penn Common, seen here at the time of the tenancy of William Henry Priest in the 1930s, by 1840. A previous landlord, William Lloyd Roberts, built some houses which survive to this day on the Common.

Compton Farm and the smaller Lodge Farm. The latter has recently been restored but the site of the pub is now occupied by housing set back from the road.

ANOTHER LANDLORD WITH PROPERTY AMBITIONS was Roland Ray who erected twelve houses close to his Pheasant Inn, Oldbury. The woodland setting of the pub, which doubled as a farm, attracted many visitors from Bearwood on summer evenings.

THE HALF WAY HOUSE at Tettenhall stands exactly halfway between London and Holyhead on the main road between the capital and the chief sea port to Ireland. This thoroughfare was greatly improved by Thomas Telford, who also undertook much canal engineering work throughout the Black Country.

THE GLOBE in Pleck, over 300 years old, once stood in open countryside. In the 1850s it was also a farm with the 80 acres being run by the licensee. Soon after this the Clews family bought the pub and ran it for over 30 years. The pub had a skittle alley and also saw the less innocent pastimes of dog fighting and cock fighting. The smithy was used as a mortuary for anyone who fell in the canal and drowned. Pictured here in 1954, the pub had continued its home brewing until 1916.

THE OLD FIELD HOUSE, which stood in Tettenhall's Codsall Road, owed its name to a medieval farming system. Later rebuilt, its more recent name, The Claregate (after its locality), helps to avoid confusion with The Field House at nearby Wightwick.

DRINKING UP TIME meant something quite different for customers at the isolated Victory Cave Inn on Bentley Common in April 1951. Excavations for the proposed railway sidings for the local power station had weakened the hundred year old building, and long-time landlord Isaacher Pearsall was told by the licensing justices that he had to close immediately the last of his beer stocks was finished.

BEFORE THE MASSIVE HOUSING PROGRAMME of the period between the two World Wars a very large area called the Uplands stood to the right of The Old Chapel Inn, Smethwick. This land had been open countryside with several farms and large houses. Old Chapel also lay to the west. The pub dates from about 1800. Smethwick Old Church, built in 1732, is behind it.

THIS WOMBOURNE PUB, dating from before the turn of the century is in Ounsdale Road. It was owned by Darby's, most of whose pubs were closer than this to their brewery in Greets Green. The pub is pictured in the early 1950s.

THE RAVEN in Wordesley, at the Belle View end of Bells Lane, once offered 'Noted Home Brewed Ales'. The pub still has a bowling green.

CHARLES CROWTHER kept this woodland setting tourist attraction in Penn on the corner of Church Hill and Penn Road from 1904 to 1908. The horse-drawn bus travelled the two-to-three mile journey from Wolverhampton five times a day until the service ceased in 1911. Subsidence necessitated the pub's demolition and rebuilding in 1980. The original building had previously been rebuilt in the 1930s.

THIS TWO-HUNDRED-YEAR-OLD LANGLEY GREEN PUB, set amid greens and heaths, still retains a feeling of its former rural location. In the nineteenth century its landlords not only maintained the pub but also ran the adjoining smithy which served the numerous local farms.

THIS HART'S HILL PUB closed down in 1975 after passing through the ownership of four different breweries.

SECTION EIGHT

Names

The naming of pubs has always been an important matter. Long ago landlords became tired of repeatedly changing their pub's name to that of the newly crowned monarch and, to show royalist allegiance, simply adopted the name 'The Crown'. The pub's name could be that of its locality – Shireland, Neachells, Thimble Mill – or reflect local activities. The Pheasant, The Dog and Partridge, The Hare and Hounds were named for the local game hunting.

The Black Country, so rich in trade and industry, had a wealth of pub names to show which workers they were built to serve – The Miners Arms, The Jolly Collier, The Farriers. Local landmarks would become the pub's name – Five Ways, The Stone Cross, The Yew Tree. Local families had their names enshrined in pub names – The Scott Arms, The Pipe Vaults, The Bradford Arms.

Perhaps best of all are the nicknames, ingenious, funny and so well known that eventually they might become the official name. The Crooked House was orginally The Glynne Arms. The Hole was the nickname for a pub in a hollow. The Widders was a pub kept by a widow. How many drinkers at The Bull and Bladder remember they are actually in The Vine, or those in Ma Pardoe's realise they are in fact in The Old Swan. Often the origin of the pub's nickname is lost and can only be guessed at; there are a number of theories as to why The Frying Pan is so called.

Stage coaches stopped at inns for overnight shelter and refreshment in the days of long uncomfortable journeys; the name of the pub they were approaching must have been on the minds of the weary travellers. So integral are pubs to the local community and so much do they become a landmark in themselves, that they are often used as staging posts when giving directions for a journey. Even now, in the days of demolition and rebuilding of pubs, the name is usually carefully preserved to live on in the new premises.

The pubs mentioned above are to be found throughout this book; this section deals with names which are particularly unusual or intriguing.

THE JOLLY COLLIER was a name given to many Black Country pubs by landlords hoping to attract the custom of their local mining communities. A typical example is this Brades Village pub, pictured here in July 1962.

NAIL MAKING was another major Black Country industry, but in this instance The Jolly Nailer was built and named by the customers, Welsh nailers who had moved into the Lyndon area near today's Sandwell General Hospital.

LOCAL INDUSTRIAL CONNECTIONS were further emphasized by calling pubs after mechanical equipment. The Brownhills pub (left) was named after a ram used in pile-driving operations. A once common pub sign showed people overcoming life's difficulties; sometimes this portrayed a man carrying a woman on his back. Moxley's The Struggler (right) in Church Street was possibly previously called The Struggling Man. The Old Wilkin is now a restaurant, but the Joules house has disappeared.

THIS APPROPRIATELY NAMED PUB was built opposite James Watt's famous 1796 Soho Foundry, Foundry Lane, Smethwick. Toiling in hot and demanding conditions, foundry workers were known to consume vast quantities of ale.

THE MILLARD FAMILY brewed their own beer until the 1950s. Originally called The Jolly Collier, this Dudley pub was renamed to avoid confusion with similarly named pubs reflecting the local mining industry. Apparently a nearby gipsies' camp inspired the new name.

THE HOP AND BARLEY CORN was in Mason Street, Coseley and has since been rebuilt. Just as 'The Vine' or 'Bunch of Grapes' celebrate wine, so many pub names, such as 'The Hop Pole' or 'The Barley Mow', extolled the virtues of beer.

THE HARMONIC, on the corner of Church Street and West Bromwich Street, Oldbury, was in existence from at least the 1880s. Its name meant harmonious and agreeable, most appropriate for a pub! Pictured here in April 1961, it has since been demolished.

DERIVING ITS NAME from its previous use as a butchers, this very old Tettenhall pub was rebuilt in 1980.

DANIEL HOLLOWAY, a coal dealer by trade, also built houses and cottages. The home he built for himself in Halfords Lane, Smethwick in the 1840s became a pub after he had lived in it for about twenty years – and was given a very appropriate name! One of its licensees was the former Albion full-back and England cap, Billy Williams.

THIS PUB, although actually in Quarry Bank's Maughan Street, was built very close to The Bower, the old name for the western end of the street. Park Road is now the name for what was once the upper part of Bower Lane. The pub was demolished in the late 1980s and the site later offered for housing development.

J.L. MOILLET, a Swiss merchant, sold part of his Smethwick Grove Estate to provide a site for the London Works, an engineering company which was later involved in major projects including the Crystal Palace.

THE LONG-ESTABLISHED PIPE FAMILY, landowners in Bilston, lent their name to many local landmarks, including The Pipe Vaults pictured here in the 1950s. A distinguished member of the family was Richard Pipe, London's Lord Mayor in 1578.

THIS PUB'S NAME is taken from the district of Wolverhampton in which it stands. Necheles, Nechels, and Nechells, were all various forms of spelling for an ancient word meaning homestead.

IVAN STEPANOVICH MAZEPPA was a Polish nobleman and Cossack soldier who later fought for the Swedish King Charles XII in 1709. Mazeppa's amorous adventures inspired Lord Byron to write a poem about him. The poem, published in 1819, must have caught the public's imagination, as a number of pubs were given his name. This photograph of Wednesbury's Mazeppa was taken in Elwell Street in July 1962.

Then and Now

There is a particular sadness when an old familiar building disappears and is replaced by a modern structure. That feeling is all the more acute when an old pub goes with all the memories of a happy, often cosy place. Whatever the replacement, if there is one, it may be some time before the new premises acquire a sense of familiarity.

Most examples in this section show small pubs being replaced by large establishments. Other photographs illustrate attempts to give a pub a facelift; in some cases the approach is more subtle with new lettering and a splash of paint, a move cheaper than rebuilding.

THE SPON CROFT (above) at the Smethwick end of Spon Lane was replaced in 1935 by the newer premises erected on the opposite side of the street, visible to the left in the top photograph.

AT THE NAGS HEAD, Great Bridge the brewery effected less dramatic change by the judicious use of paint.

THE SEVEN STARS, once part of a Bilston farm, was totally transformed by its 1934 rebuilding.

THE OLD COURT HOUSE, built at Kingswinford by the Earl of Dudley in the late 1700s, doubled as a public house and a meeting place for the local manorial court. The top picture shows the pub at the beginning of this century prior to its later new 'old half-timbering'.

THE HIGH STREET PORCH ENTRANCE is visible on the left in this view, taken on the corner of Stony Lane, Smethwick, of The Blue Gates prior to its 1930 demolition. The replacement, which opened on 7 October 1932, is viewed below from Stony Lane. (See p. 106.)

COUNTRY COTTAGE CHARM made way in July 1932 for the opening of The Two Brewers, Queens Road, Smethwick. This pub, along with The Abbey and The Thimble Mill, was purpose-built to meet the increase in trade resulting from the large scale housing developments taking place around this time.

THE COCK INN, Brasshouse Lane, Smethwick, in November 1939 (above) and almost a quarter of a century later in July 1962 (below). The newer premises have since been closed but, being near to the recently restored Smethwick Pumping Station, it is planned to convert them into a canal interpretation centre within the Galton Valley Park.

THE ROYAL OAK, Langley Green, has been updated by some slight structural alterations and repainting carried out by the brewery.

SUBTLE REFURBISHMENT carried out at a Smethwick corner pub.

WEDNESBURY'S OLD GEORGE HOTEL is pictured above in April 1958. Dating from coaching days, when it was known as The King's Head, the pub was the venue for a murder trial in the long hot summer of 1844. John Jeavons was once landlord, followed by Simeon Constable, both of whom came from old Wednesbury families. Below is shown its early 1960s replacement.

AN UNUSUAL REAR VIEW OF A TINY PUB. Also unusually, the Cape Hill area of Smethwick took its name from The Cape of Good Hope pub – a more general practice was for licensed premises to borrow their names from their locality. Below, the new pub in August 1930, five years after construction.

SECTION TEN

Fun at the Pub

In the hard working days of the early nineteenth century the pub provided a place in which to forget the toil of industry and the squalor of home life. It was also customary for wages to be paid out on Saturday nights in the pub where the landlord obligingly laid on plenty of food and good ale.

Aside from the chapel, there was no other institution better placed to organize recreational events than the pub. It was often the venue for the official business of a community: magistrates and coroners held court; football clubs (Wolves used The Molineux as a dressing room) and local societies met there; religious services sometimes took place (even as late as 1948 at The Stone Cross near West Bromwich), and on land adjoining The Moilliet Arms there was a two-day Smethwick 'wake' and later funfair.

During official celebrations such as royal jubilees the larger pubs dutifully decorated themselves for the occasion. A children's tea party at The Cottage Spring, Crookhay Lane, West Bromwich on Coronation Day in 1953 showed how the smaller establishments could join in such fun. Outings from pubs provided the local photographer with a steady income as everybody usually bought a copy of the photograph of the line-up outside as the party prepared to go on its way.

The traditional pub games of darts, bowls, skittles, cribbage, dominoes and quoits abounded amid the gatherings of the pigeon fanciers. Other more unusual groups such as the 'Fryin' Pon Club' met at Darlaston's Bradford Arms and the Clay Pipe Club at The White Horse in Cradley Heath. All this goes to prove that the pub was and still is more than a place to go for just a drink!

IN THE PRINCE REGENT, Horseley Heath, the licensee's budgerigar Joey perches on a pint in March 1954. Joey also used to sit on the heads, hands or shoulders of customers. Behind, the mirror of the neatly arranged bar reflects the photographer's camera and hands.

WILLIAM BEASLEY, Tipton's 'Memory Man', in The Britannia in April 1954. Mr Beasley earned his nickname with his amazing ability to recall sporting facts and figures. He explained that as he was so interested in sport he seemed able to recall all he read. On quiz nights his answers to questions on football, racing and boxing could be checked out as correct in the record books. The Britannia, in Tipton's Lower Church Lane, had originally been two small cottages, converted into a pub well over 150 years ago. In 1975 it was renamed The Black Country Man as there were two other Britannias in the area.

A CELEBRATION GATHERING for the silver jubilee of George V and Queen Mary in 1935 at this Walsall beerhouse dating from 1834. It was later owned by the Evans Brewery Ltd, Perry Barr. In 1933 G.S. Twist set up his brewery which continued production of the famous White Horse minerals even after the 1950 Atkinson's takeover of his twenty pubs. This Wolverhampton Street Inn closed in 1975.

THE MARKET is still in place outside The Limerick, Great Bridge in August 1969. Built in 1837, the pub has seen many changes to the roadways outside. The nearby section of the Black Country Spine Road was completed in 1990, with the main road running to the right and a service road to the left. The market is now held in Mill Street.

THE BOWLS TEAM of The Royal Oak, Tettenhall, which included many members of a long-established family of local builders, the Daltons. Bearded John Dalton sits next to suited landlord Horace Batkin. Seated far right is the pub's brewer, Joe Williams, known locally for obvious reasons as 'The Brewer'. The bowling green behind the pub was towards the top end of Cow (now Shaw) Lane.

FUNFAIR RIDES set up on the High Street, Cradley Heath, outside The Holly Bush, where landlords Nenemiah Homer, father and son, kept the pub over a fifty-year period.

DANCING FOR JOY outside the richly decorated Sandwell Hotel, High Street, West Bromwich. It is generally agreed that this photograph was taken in 1902 at the time of King Edward VII's coronation.

THE VINE, Walsall, decorated for another royal occasion, a jubilee of Queen Victoria. Built at the corner of Caldmore Road and Lower Hall Street, Walsall, this eighteenth-century pub was rebuilt in the 1940s.

PROMINENTLY PLACED on Dudley's High Street, this establishment, built in 1786 and replacing The Rose and Crown of the 1600s, played a leading role for many years in the life of the community. This particular crowd had gathered for the 1886 election victory of Brooke Robinson as the town's Conservative MP. The hotel was demolished in 1968 to provide a site for Marks and Spencer.

LICENSEE GEORGE WILLETTS is posing in the doorway of The Fountain Inn, Holloway Bank in about 1898. In front of him is his daughter, who died in 1977, aged 85. Thomas Telford's road improvements in 1820 left the pub standing below the level of the road. The pub was replaced in the 1930s by the present much higher building. 'Good stabling', advertised on the top left corner of the pub, was important on this main stage-coach road to Holyhead.

A PRE-FIRST WORLD WAR PICTURE of customers gathered together outside Pelsall's Swan Inn. At the time the pub was being run by George Rogers.

REGULARS pose at the rear of The Talbot, Digbeth, Walsall, where a verandah passage conveniently permitted the consumption of ale. This old building closed in January 1962 for the erection of new premises.

A GROUP OF TIPTON FOOTBALLERS lined up at The Miners Arms, Owen Street, Tipton in December 1956 – the time of James Dean's success in *Rebel Without a Cause*.

READY FOR THE START OF AN OUTING from The Bridge Inn, Wolverhampton Road, Walsall. Originally a beerhouse, it was acquired in 1925 by local brewer John Lord of Shortacre Street. The pub was rebuilt in 1939, the year of the brewery's takeover by Mitchells & Butlers Ltd.

A GAME OF CRIBBAGE between landlord Lew Poxon and customer 'Taffy' at The Prince Albert, Moor Street, West Bromwich.

FORMER BREWER SID SMITH sits third from the left watching a game of cards in progress at The Cottage Spring in February 1965. This Franchise Street pub was the last in Wednesbury to brew its own ale.

A BACHELOR PARTY at Dudley's Little Barrel, 26 April 1953.

A CORONATION PARTY IN FULL SWING in the yard of The Cottage Spring, Crookhay Lane, West Bromwich in June 1953.

LINE-UP FOR A COACH OUTING from Great Bridge's Stork Inn.

BRAVE SMILING FACES on the last Saturday at The Dudley Arms Hotel, 11 May 1968. Despite being a listed building it was demolished to provide a High Street site for Marks and Spencer. Some years later the Dudley store was closed and re-opened in new premises at the Merry Hill centre.

FLOODS IN NEWHAMPTON ROAD, Wolverhampton in 1914 – more fun for the children than the adults! The pub was delicensed and the building reopened about a year later as a branch of the Samaritans on 3 September 1986.

THREE AND A HALF FEET OF WATER flooded out customers and caused the loss of over £100 worth of stock at 'The Hole' (the local nickname for this pub because of its location in a hollow) on Sunday 21 August 1966. A greater disaster of a different kind nearly occurred

twenty-two years earlier when a German bomb which failed to explode fell on part of the wall enclosing the area fronting the pub. Originally called The James Bridge Hotel until the coming of the railway to Darlaston, it was refurbished in 1988.

THE BLUE BALL, Old Hill, on Sunday 1 March 1964, an important day for the pub's Pigeon Club with the holding of the annual auction sale of the Midlands Federation of Pigeon Flying Clubs. Officiating was the Federation Secretary G.H. Homer, with Edgar Glaze, Vice President, and J.W. Shakspeare, Chairman, acting as auctioneers. Mr Frank George, the millionaire Chairman of Weetabix, paid the day's best price of £6 10s. for an egg.

A FORMAL – AND FULLY EQUIPPED – GATHERING of the Pipe Club at The White Horse, Cradley Heath. The occasion was the Coronation Day celebrations for George V on 22 June 1911.

INDEX